Becoming Your
DOG'S BEST FRIEND

How To Earn Your Dog's Love

BY
MARTIN J. BECKER, DVM

Illustrated By Molly Pearce

Dedication

I've flourished because of the unconditional love of my wife Teresa, my children Mikkel and Lex, my parents Bob and Virginia, and our Wirehaired Fox Terrier "Scooter". Thousands of dogs have touched my life both as a veterinarian and as a pet owner. With this book I hope to return to dogs a small portion of what they have so unselfishly and generously given us.

Distributed in the UNITED STATES to the Pet Trade by T.F.H. Publications, Inc., One T.F.H. Plaza, Neptune City, NJ 07753; distributed in the UNITED STATES to the Bookstore and Library Trade by National Book Network, Inc. 4720 Boston Way, Lanham MD 20706; in CANADA to the Pet Trade by H & L Pet Supplies Inc., 27 Kingston Crescent, Kitchener, Ontario N2B 2T6; Rolf C. Hagen Ltd., 3225 Sartelon Street, Montreal 382 Quebec; in CANADA to the Book Trade by Macmillan of Canada (A Division of Canada Publishing Corporation), 164 Commander Boulevard, Agincourt, Ontario M1S 3C7; in ENGLAND by T.F.H. Publications, PO Box 15, Waterlooville PO7 6BQ; in AUSTRALIA AND THE SOUTH PACIFIC by T.F.H. (Australia), Pty. Ltd., Box 149, Brookvale 2100 N.S.W., Australia; in NEW ZEALAND by Brooklands Aquarium Ltd. 5 McGiven Drive, New Plymouth, RD1 New Zealand; in Japan by T.F.H. Publications, Japan—Jiro Tsuda, 10-12-3 Ohjidai, Sakura, Chiba 285, Japan; in SOUTH AFRICA by Multipet Pty. Ltd., P.O. Box 35347, Northway, 4065, South Africa. Published by T.F.H. Publications, Inc.
MANUFACTURED IN THE UNITED STATES OF AMERICA
BY T.F.H. PUBLICATIONS, INC.

CONTENTS

Introduction

One of life's greatest experiences is not having a dog, but loving a dog. Dogs provide unconditional, limitless affection and "to die for" loyalty. No longer relegated to the backyard, dogs have become extended family members that are nurtured, loved and protected. We talk to them, carry photos in our wallets of them, celebrate birthdays with them, buy Christmas gifts for them and sleep with them.

There is something wonderful between people and pets called the human/animal bond that is stronger and more different than anything else in nature. It is a magical chemistry that has intrigued and delighted the human race for centuries. Archaeologists have documented that the dog was the first animal to be domesticated, at least 10,500 years ago. Primitive man used dogs to carry loads and to help in hunting. Then, somewhere in the void of time, man petted a dog, the dog wagged his tail in appreciation, and the precious human/animal bond was born.

The companionship of a faithful four legged friend not only makes you feel good...it can also be good for you. They provide consistency, stability, entertainment, an emotional outlet, a means of stress reduction and a method of socialization. *No wonder dogs are man's best friend!*

It takes less than a day for a new puppy to form an inseparable link with a new family. Once set, this emotional bond is nearly impossible to break, although guide dogs and hearing dogs can break and remake very strong bonds two to three times in a lifetime! This bond consists of friendship, companionship and complete acceptance.

Dogs lend a touch of graciousness to all our lives because they tend to bring out the kindest and most generous impulses of humanity. Dogs promote a state of peaceful coexistence between humans and the rest of creation. They keep

us from believing that we, and the material things around us, are the be-all and end-all of the earth.

The love affair between man and dogs has gone on for tens of thousands of years and it is becoming more important by the day.

Humans need dogs. We need their devotion and unconditional love. The question we must consider is: Do we understand the commitment a dog requires from us and are we returning to them the devotion we owe?

PET OWNERSHIP ON THE RISE

According to a recent study conducted by Brady Associates, a New York communications firm specializing in the pet industry, five factors point towards an increase in pet ownership in the 1990 s!

• **The need for companionship is growing.** As people live longer and, more often, alone, pets are prime companions.

• **Family values are becoming more important.** With the resurgence of traditional values and the growing dissatisfaction with the American school system, more parents are seeing pet ownership as a way to teach their children responsibility.

• **There is a greater need to reassert control over one's life.** As people sense a loss of control over their jobs, the government and the economy, pet ownership provides an element of stability and control.

• **Pet ownership is becoming a more socially acceptable means of self-expression.** Unlike the self-indulgent "me" attitude of the 80s, the 90s will manifest themselves in the "we" attitude of sensitivity, caring and warmth.

• **The quality of interpersonal relationships is declining.** For various reasons, the quality of human relationships is deteriorating. People will increasingly compensate for unsatisfactory human relationships by seeking the unconditional and abundant love of their dog.

That Wonderful Thing Called the Human/Animal Bond

The therapeutic, emotional and social roles of dogs are expanding. As family, neighbor and community bonds diminish, the human/animal bond is strengthening. Having "someone" to care for gives meaning to life: a reason to get up in the morning, a reason to want to come home at night. Dogs satisfy the need to be needed and loved, an emotion that runs deep in all of us, regardless of age, color, sex or economic success.

Will Rogers may have said it best: "No man can be condemned for owning a dog. As long as he's got a dog, he's got a friend and the poorer he gets the better friend he has."

People go to outrageous lengths to show their pets love. Sensible or not, we all have "our ways" of showing our love. But there can be no real love without responsibility. We all share a responsibility to be kind to dogs, to prevent their pain, suffering and unnecessary death and to keep them happy and healthy. Consider it a repayment for their devotion and contribution to the welfare of all humankind.

Ten Steps for Being a Perfect Pet Partner

1) I feed my dog a high-quality food, I give him nutritious snacks and I watch his weight.
2) I give my dog all the fresh, clean water he wants at all times.
3) I exercise my dog everyday and when out of my yard, I always use a leash.
4) I play with my dog everyday and never hurt him intentionally.
5) I have safe toys for my dog and at the end of the day, I pick them up and put them away.
6) I keep my dog bathed, brushed and beautiful.
7) I will teach my dog basic obedience and will give him loving discipline.
8) I will housetrain my dog, keep him off the furniture and away from dangerous products and places.
9) I will take my dog to the veterinarian for regular check-ups and inoculations.
10) I will always be compassionate with my dog; when he hurts, I will hurt.

"We all share a resonsibility to be kind to dogs, to prevent their pain, suffering and unnecessary death and to keep them happy and healthy."

Are You Ready for a Dog?

Experts on people/pet behavior say a dog can provide a person or a family with a close companion, playmate and reliable friend.

Remember, though, a dog is a big commitment of resources for the entire family. A commitment of time, energy and money. Never buy a dog on impulse or without knowing all the facts! First, gather enough information to make an informed decision.

Properly chosen, trained and nurtured, a dog can be a loved and loving member of your family for years to come. But first, you must learn to be a responsible pet owner.

GOOD REASONS TO GET A DOG

• Dogs love unconditionally. They don't criticize or give orders and they are good listeners.

• Dogs can be good for you both physically and emotionally.

• People can gain self-esteem and a sense of worth from owning and caring for a dog.

• A dog teaches patience and responsibility.

• A dog teaches the importance of rules and limits.

• A dog is fun to play and exercise with.

GOOD REASONS NOT TO GET A DOG

• You're not allowed to have dogs where you live.

• You don't have an outside area to exercise your pet daily.

• You're not willing or able to exercise your pet daily or take the time for proper training.

• Dogs require more care, attention and training than other pets; duties that may be difficult for busy families.

• Dogs require a certain amount of money that is budgeted for their care and well-being. This includes food, grooming, veterinary care and obedience training.

• If your child has allergies, or if there is a family history

"Never buy a dog on impulse or without knowing all the facts!"

of them, have the child tested for allergies to dogs. With precautions, your child may still be able to enjoy a dog!

• You are not willing to be a responsible pet owner.

"Dogs require more care, attention and training than other pets; duties that may be difficult for busy families."

WHY PEOPLE NEED PETS

They provide companionship.
They give us something to care for.
They provide pleasurable activity.
They are a source of constancy in our changing lives.
They make us feel safe.
They return us to play and laughter.
They are a stimulus to exercise.
They comfort us with touch.
They are pleasurable to watch.

From: *Between Pets and People*
By Dr. Alan Beck and Dr. Aaron Katcher

Being a Responsible Dog Owner

A responsible pet owner is someone who loves his pet unconditionally and does anything and everything necessary to keep his pet happy and healthy.

Responsible dog owners *provide* for the basic needs of their pet (food, water, grooming, medical care, etc.) and lavish love and attention on them.

They *protect* the health, safety and happiness of their pet, as well as that of their neighbors and their community.

Responsible owners *prevent* their pets from roaming free, producing unwanted litters, unnecessarily suffering or dying prematurely. Free-roaming pets face many dangers (cars, other animals and disease) and can cause many problems (biting, breeding and destroying property). Responsible pet owners keep their pets inside or control their pets with a fence, a run, a trolley or a

"The decision to buy a pet is a big one and the commitment to care for a pet properly is even bigger. "

leash at *all* times. If their pet is ever lost, a permanent identification tattoo, tag or microchip will help them return home quickly and safely. You should also keep a current photo and a current record of your dog's age, weight, height and markings.

The decision to buy a pet is a big one and the commitment to care for a pet properly is even bigger. Before your buy or adopt a pet you must be 110% ready to honor that commitment and responsibility for your pet's entire life.

"Usually kids want to help take care of the new puppy. The fact is, they need to help!"

MAKING RESPONSIBLE PET OWNERSHIP A FAMILY AFFAIR

Usually kids *want* to help take care of the new puppy. The fact is, they *need* to help! Shouldering part of the workload, both the fun and not so fun chores, is a valuable exercise in responsibility.

Together, over the course of your pet's lifetime, you will feel the worry of sickness or injury, the consequences of irresponsibility and eventually the sorrow of death.

There are no hard and fast rules about how much responsibility children should be expected to take with a pet. Even with "my pet" there should be "family responsibility." Here are some basic guidelines on what to expect from children:

Preschoolers—an adult should be present at all times, but the child can help fill the food and water dishes, help walk the dog, help go the veterinarian, etc.

Ages 5-8—can fill the food and water dishes and clean up the yard without supervision and can bathe and brush the pet's coat with some occasional help. By the age of seven to eight, the child should remember to do the basics without being told—but you will still need to remind him occasionally.

Ages 9-12—can handle almost all the chores necessary to take care of the pet: food, water, exercise, bathing, yard detail, etc. A child needs to understand the negative consequences to the pet if he forgets to keep the water dish full, for example.

Teenagers—can take full responsibility for a pet including knowing that something "just isn't right" with the dog. Trips to the veterinarian at this age sometimes lead to career choices!

CAN YOU AFFORD TO BE A RESPONSIBLE PET OWNER?

Although your actual expenses depend on many factors (did you pay for a dog or adopt a stray, purebred or mongrel, big or small, long coat or coat that needs professional grooming, indoor, outdoor, etc.), the following list may help you decide if you can budget enough money to take care of a pet properly. Don't forget you'll still need money for occasional emergencies and unforeseen expenses!

- Purchase price
- Vaccinations, veterinary care and maintenance (parasite control, dental care, etc.)
- Supplies (bowls, leash, collar, ID tag, therapeutic chew toys, Nylabone® products, grooming products, etc.)
- Microchip ID implant
- Food (per year)
- Grooming (if applicable)

"Don't forget you'll still need money for occasional emergencies and unforeseen expenses!

Choosing Your Dog

In some ways, choosing a dog is similar to choosing a family car. You can pick from a variety of types, colors and sizes but only you will know which one is just right for *you*.

However, there is a major difference. A dog is a living being whose life your family will shape, share and nurture. Your dog will be an important part of the family for years to come. Therefore, you must consider the traits of the selected dog and the lifestyle and commitment of your family.

When choosing the best pet for you or your family, the most important considerations are the ages and personalities of your children, your lifestyle and the breed, temperament, habits and age of the dog. Give your choice careful consideration. Your decision must stand the test of time.

PUPPY OR ADULT

Puppies are often the most desirable new pets, since their personalities are shaped by their early socialization. Puppies and children can grow up together.

Puppies between eight to ten weeks of age are the most receptive and adaptable to human families although, for very young children, a young adult dog might be a better choice. Toddlers might not understand that a puppy is fragile and needs special care.

CROSSBRED OR PUREBRED

A purebred dog is born of genetically similar parents—the same "breed." The term crossbred means that the dogs is the offspring of genetically

different parents—a hybrid. Is a purebred or a crossbred dog the best? Some behaviorists say that mixed-breed dogs are often healthier and temperamentally more stable, but a purebred's physical traits are more predictable. Understand, however, that even purebred breeds can change over time and vary by region. Also individual dogs' personalities vary, regardless of breed! If you've had a purebred dog in the past, that's usually what you tend to get again, same for mixed-breeds. Usually it's a matter of personal preference.

YOUR PERFECT NEW DOG

Imagine the perfect dog for you. It would love you, play

with you and share your secrets! It might very well become your "best friend"!

Dogs come in all sizes, colors and temperaments. In fact, there are almost 500 different kinds of dogs and each breed has a certain appearance or personality. And there are millions of mixed-breed dogs that are just as bright, beautiful and loving as purebred dogs.

Choosing the right dog is an important decision and requires a lot of thought and study. Just because a dog is cute and friendly doesn't mean that he will fit into your family's home and lifestyle. For example, large dogs with long coats need a lot of space, exercise and care. Whereas, smaller dogs with short coats that don't shed can do just fine in an apartment. So while the choice of the "perfect new

"Although our heart usually tells us which dog is "just right" for us, it helps to know a few telltale signs for health and sickness."

PUPPY SIGNS

Sickness	Health
Lifeless, runny eyes.	Energetic, bright eyes.
Runny or dry nose.	Wet cool nose.
Dull or uneven coat with a lot of shedding or dander.	Glossy, full coat.
Scratching.	
Ears are red and/or smelly or are filled with black waxy material.	Clean pink ears.
Listless and not playful.	Energetic, alert, playful.
Soft or runny stool, blood in stool.	Firm, well-formed stool.
Thin but pot bellied (worms).	Seems well proportioned.
Limps, doesn't eat, cries in pain	Active, good appetite.

- Do I want a dog I can hold in my lap and pet? (This usually means a small friendly dog.)

- Do I want an outdoor dog? (Depending on the climate and the breed this usually means a bigger, hardier dog.)

- Do I have a big yard? (Large active dogs need a lot of space.)

- Do I want a dog that likes to play? (Some breeds like to play, others are less energetic.)

- Can I put up with some mess? (Puppies must be housebroken, longhaired breeds shed, etc.)

"Choosing the right dog is an important decision and requires a lot of thought and study."

friend" can be mind-boggling, always approach it honestly and logically.

CHOOSING A HEALTHY DOG

Although our heart usually tells us which dog is "just right" for us, it helps to know a few telltale signs for health and sickness. When you go comparison shopping for a pet, you can use the "Puppy Signs" checklist to help guide your final decision, a decision based on equal parts of emotion and logic!

OTHER POINTS TO CONSIDER

"Unless you're used to handling and training dogs, avoid aggressive breeds."

- Avoid breeds whose physical characteristics (long hair, large size, high exercise requirement, etc.) clash with your lifestyle or budget.
- Small dogs can get hurt in rough play with children and large dogs can sometimes frighten or injure small children.
- Unless you're used to handling and training dogs, avoid aggressive breeds.
- Energetic dogs take a lot of strength and can accidentally hurt a child.
- Some purebred dogs run a higher risk of genetic defects.
- A large dog can cost three to six times as much to feed as a small one.
- Most experts feel female dogs are less aggressive.
- If possible, examine the litter. An energetic and

playful but nondominant puppy usually makes a better pet than either the "top dog" or the timid runt of the litter.

• Know community laws and responsibilities regarding leash laws, vaccination requirements and licensing.

Consult your veterinarian and local animal behaviorists *before* you make a final choice. Your veterinarian is a pet health expert and will counsel you on breed characteristics, genetic problems, health problems, estimated annual costs for preventative health care, grooming, feeding and any other special needs. You should also talk with local breeders and trainers.

"Small dogs can get hurt in rough play with children."

QUESTIONS TO ASK BEFORE YOU BUY

• Age, sex, and breed(s) of dog?

• If a purebred, is the dog registered and can you get papers?

• Temperament and bad habits of mother and father?

• What vaccinations has the dog had? What vaccinations has the mother had?

• Has the dog been wormed or checked for worms?

• What is the dog eating (brand, dry or canned, etc.), how often and how much?

• If old enough, has the dog been spayed or neutered?

• Is the dog housebroken and does he exhibit any other destructive behavior such as biting, barking, digging, chewing?

THE OPTION OF ADOPTION

Most people find purebred dogs through friends, neighbors, or newspaper ads. Given the large number of abandoned and unwanted animals, please first consider adopting a homeless pet from your local humane society or animal shelter. This can be a reliable, humane and inexpensive source for mixed-breed dogs that need a loving home.

Picking out your dog is something you will never forget. Having done your research, let your child pick out the dog, but agree that you have the final say because sometimes children will pick out sick, overly aggressive, nervous or timid pets.

SOME DOGS...

Some dogs hate to be alone.
Some dogs have an uneven temperament.
Some dogs are high-strung.
Some dogs need an even ambient temperature.
Some dogs tend to bite if startled.
Some dogs hate to be handled.
Some dogs tend to roam.
Some dogs don't do well with other animals or dogs of the same or opposite sex.

Preparing for Your Pet's First Days at Home

Seven important things that every dog needs are:

1) Food—Nutritionally complete in just the right amounts.

2) Water—Clean and fresh at all times.

3) Shelter—A clean, secure place of refuge.

4) Grooming—Keeps your dog clean, healthy, happy and handsome.

5) Exercise—Keeps your dog physically fit, healthy and happy.

6) Veterinary care—Although educated, trained and prepared to handle accidents and treat illnesses, your veterinarian will concentrate on preventive health care programs to keep your pet happy and healthy.

7) Love, affection and fun—Just like humans, pets thrive on friendship, companionship, trust, love and fun!

Once you've decided on a particular pet, there are certain things your pet will require such as food, external parasite control, grooming supplies, chew toys and odor-control products that are best purchased *before* you bring your new puppy home. Other items such as collars, leashes and ID tags are best purchased *after* you pick up

"There are certain things your pet will require that are best purchased before you bring your new puppy home."

your pet. It is recommended that you consult your veterinarian on these items. At the same time the veterinarian will set up the preventive health care program that will keep your new friend happy, healthy and long-lived. In doing this you'll be off to a good start towards many years of rewarding companionship and devotion.

PUPPY-PROOFING YOUR HOME

You will need to get down on your hands and knees and scour the pet's living area for poisons, sharp objects, small objects that can be swallowed and other potential dangers.

Some suggestions for a puppy-proof home:

Don't leave cigarette butts where puppy can reach

"You will need to get down on your hands and knees and scour the pet's living area for potential dangers."

them. If eaten, they can lead to nicotine toxicity.

Secure electrical cords to baseboards or make them inaccessible. If your puppy chews a cord, severe electrical burns or even death may result!

Keep decorations up high or keep inaccessible. Your pet may chew and swallow something that will harm him.

Never burn candles where they are accessible. Pups are attracted to them and may get burned.

Keep medication bottles inaccessible. Even child-proof containers are no match for a dog's strong jaws.

Keep the toilet lid down if you use toilet bowl cleaners. They are strongly alkaline and can burn your pet's intestinal tract or make him sick.

Keep basement doors and windows closed. A curious puppy may have a tragic accident.

Don't expose your puppy to other dogs or even other people, since they can carry virus with them, until your puppy is fully protected by vaccinations.

Don't give your pet natural bones. Dispose of bones in a manner that is inaccessible. They can be fatal! Dogs should be provided safe alternatives, such as a Nylabone® or Gumabone®.

Don't leave needles, splinters, pins or yarn where they are accessible. They are often swallowed, sometimes with tragic results.

Be certain antifreeze (and other poisons) are inaccessible and any drippings are cleaned up immediately. Antifreeze smells sweet and dogs are often attracted to it, usually with fatal results. Antifreeze is highly toxic; only a few drops can kill!

Use insecticides, pesticides, herbicides and rodenticides with moderation and extreme caution.

Keep your puppy away from toxic plants and other substances. Rhododendron, Japanese Yew, poinsettias and lily of the valley can all be fatal. Such common items as peach and cherry pits or even chocolate can also be fatal in high doses. Consult your veterinarian for details.

Never give your dog any human medications, such as aspirin, without consulting your veterinarian, as they may be toxic.

TRAINING THE FAMILY FIRST

Children must understand that a puppy is not a toy but a living creature with needs and emotions. He is a playmate *not* a plaything.

Some rules to get your new friend off to a sensational start:

• Teach young children to be gentle and not pull the puppy's ear or tail. Teach them how to recognize and respond when they are holding too tightly, handling too roughly or restricting the dog from leaving.

• Don't leave children alone with the dog or puppy until they are well acquainted and know properly how to handle and care for the pet. It is recommended that children under the age of five or six only play with the dog with adult supervision.

• Make sure children wash their hands and face after playing with the dog and before eating, as puppies can carry and transmit parasites and other organisms that may be harmful to children.

• To approach any dog, teach children to walk slowly, offer the back of their hand to the dog's muzzle, speak softly and let the dog sniff. For strange dogs, children should ask an adult's permission before approaching or petting.

• Older children should be taught to hold the dog by putting one arm under the chest, the other arm under the belly near the rear legs while holding him tightly to their chest. Make sure

27

young children sit while holding the dog, as he may wiggle free and fall to the floor. Never let your child carry a dog by the scruff of the neck!

• Teach *everyone* to be considerate of the dog's needs and instincts. Pets shouldn't be disturbed when eating, sleeping or chewing, as this can provoke aggression. We all need a sanctuary, a decompression chamber, a place to "get away." Your pet is no different.

"Children must understand that a puppy is not a toy but a living creature with needs and emotions."

Caring for Your New Puppy

Not unlike a baby, your new puppy requires regular feeding, sleeping, playing and training. Of course this means that your puppy will need lots of your attention, care, time and love. Being a dog's best friend doesn't happen without commitment and dedication.

Your puppy may be frightened and apprehensive. You will want to spend a lot of time making him feel comfortable, happy and secure.

YOUR "DOGGIE DUTIES"

If you're going to be your dog's best friend, there are certain duties you must perform as needed. No exceptions! If you don't, for any reason, there will be negative consequences for your beloved friend...and maybe for you as well!

THERE'S NO PLACE LIKE HOME

When the kids are screaming and the television is blaring, your pet needs a peaceful retreat or a den all its own. For most breeds the ideal den is a crate. The crate can be made of wire or plastic

Cruel? Quite the opposite. If used properly, a crate satisfies your dog's instinctive need for a den. It is a safe sanctuary from human commotion and interference. From the dog's

MY DOGGIE DUTIES

Daily Duties
Food
Water
Vitamins
Exercise
Love

Weekly Duties
Clean up yard
Bathe and/or brush

As Needed
Trim nails
Clean crate
Clean dishes
Veterinary vists

point of view, it is not so much that he can't get out, but rather that people can't get in!

The crate also has many other valuable functions. It is a tool in housebreaking because, instinctively, a dog usually resists soiling his den. It helps prevent destructive behavior when you are away. It is also great for vacations or trips to the veterinarian.

It is important that your dog views being in the crate as a positive experience. It should be set up near the family activity center in a cozy, fairly quiet place. Remember your puppy is a baby, so throw a security blanket and a few toys inside and he's all set. It should be just big enough to permit a grown dog to stand and stretch. If it's too big, it loses it den-like qualities.

A few other things to remember:

• Don't put food or water in the crate. It is a place to

sleep, not eat.

• Start out with one to two intervals in the crate and work up to a maximum of four to five hours during the day or all night.

• Ignore your dog's crying while in the kennel and the desire to comfort it. Remember your child crying in the crib? Don't give in! Experts recommend putting a towel over the cage and sneaking up while the puppy is crying and striking the cage with your hand or a broomstick. Do it very loudly and your dog will associate his whining with a very negative stimuli of unknown origin. Soon the problem will be over!

• Never use the crate for punishment and don't put your dog in his crate after punishment. He'll be convinced that it is a place of punishment rather than a happy place of comfort and refuge.

FOOD—THE FUEL FOR HEALTH

Don't feed your dog people food. Rather than doing him a favor you may actually harm him! The need for variety in food is a human trait. Dogs don't get bored with food and frequent changes in food can make a pet finicky. Also stay with one food making sure that it is labeled as complete and appropriate for the dog's life stage and physical demands. For example, puppies, adults, geriatrics, overweight dogs and dogs with health problems generally benefit from special diets. Please consult your veterinarian, as he will give you the best advice on what to feed your dog, taking into consideration your dog's weight, age, breed, activity level, etc.

For most dogs, dry food is recommended. The nutritional value of canned and dry foods are comparable, but dry foods are more economical and convenient to buy. In addition, many veterinarians believe that dry food helps keep teeth cleaner.

Most experts now agree that until your puppy is housebroken and trained, you should keep the pet's food up and only put it down two to three times a day. Dogs have a tremendous urge to eliminate shortly after eating and this controlled feeding expedites housetraining and helps you maintain leadership.

"Please consult your veterinarian, as he will give you the best advice on what to feed your dog."

31

Once your pet is housebroken, no messes in the house for four weeks, you can start a more liberal feeding program. For small breeds, put the recommended daily portion in the bowl and let your dog eat throughout the day. For large and giant breeds, split the daily portion: one third in the morning, afternoon and evening, after six months of age: one-half in the morning and afternoon. Watch your puppy's weight and avoid overfeeding. Make sure fresh water is available at all times.

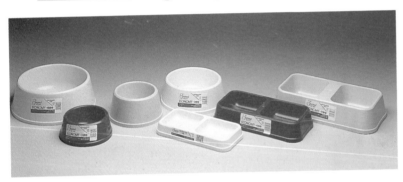

Left and below: Pet dishes come in a variety of shapes and sizes. Make sure that the dish you choose is the right size for your dog. Photos courtesy of Hagen. **Below left:** Reward your dog with 100% Beef Liver Freeze Dried Dog Treats from Gimborn.

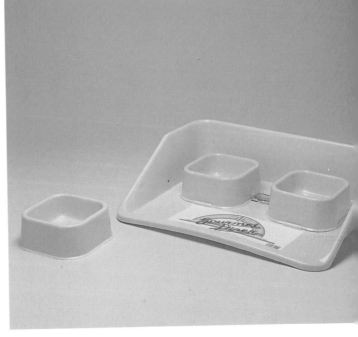

TALKING TO YOUR DOG

Almost everyone talks to their pets—99 percent in a recent survey. Eighty-five percent talk to their pets as if they were another human! However, the phenomenon of human/dog communication must be tempered with the understanding of dog behavior and obedience training.

Owners tend to misinterpret the extent of a dog's understanding when it comes to both spoken and body language. Dogs don't understand our language... but they do respond to the tone of our voice, our gestures and the emotion behind our words. Professionals recommend that you give a two-syllable name to your pet so your pet won't confuse it with one of the one-syllable basic training commands, such as sit, stay, come, down and heel. Use the two-syllable name you choose consistently. Nicknames only confuse the dog at first.

Dog training, bonding and managing are all based on the following known facts of dog behavior:

1) Dogs form social attachments known as packs. The pack works as a team in hunting for food and defending its territory. Pack behavior shows a need to be with other creatures. Living as a pet, a dog transfers this need for another animal to humans. Thus the family (or even an individual) becomes "the pack." This helps explain why dogs are such constant, loyal and dependable companions.

2) Dogs require a leader. To function efficiently, packs must exist with a minimum of conflict. Agitation is kept to a minimum by the natural tendency to have a leader and followers in every pack. There is always a pecking order in a pack. It is inevitable with your new pet that someone assumes the leadership position. Unless one of the human members is leader, your family pet will assume the role...usually with tragic consequences! Therefore, it is imperative that your dog accepts leadership from a dominant human who displays authority.

3) Dogs claim territory and create a den in the middle of it. Territory is the activity zone where a dog hunts and sleeps. The den

is a place for resting. It provides peace, comfort and security, and it is guarded with vigor! Respect your pet's privacy when inside his "special place." Don't reach in and grab the dog.

Dogs can consider their den a dog house, a crate, a room or the entire house. Rather than leave it to chance, experts recommend making the choice for the dog by providing a crate.

"Use the two syllable name you choose consistently."

Training Your Dog

Although dogs don't speak our language, their basic instinct is to please their master and accept their master as the leader. Your job as a dog's best friend, leader and responsible owner is to teach him "right from wrong," to create order from chaos and to satisfy his need for pack security. Just as small children do, pets need people to ensure their safety.

Every dog owner has a responsibility to train his pet to be a well-behaved and disciplined member not only of the home but of the neighborhood and community. Disobedient, uncontrollable dogs can be a nuisance or a menace to everyone. The result? Otherwise happy healthy dogs are often euthanized for the owner's inability or unwillingness to control problem behavior.

The secret of successful training is to train from a viewpoint that the dog can understand. Whether it's an adorable seven-week-old purebred puppy or a two-year-old mutt from the pound, you can train your dog completely and effectively once you have taught him how to please you.

Dogs understand love, praise and affection because it means you're happy! Your pet also knows when you are angry but he usually doesn't know why unless you've shown him by communicating what makes you happy. Pleasing his master, or the pack leader, is the basis for effective communication and training. Since your pet is happiest when you are happy with him, you must let him know not only what he shouldn't do but also what the acceptable alternatives are.

Understand that even the sweetest, best behaved dog will have unpleasant moments. We all do! Puppies are youngsters full of fun and mischief. Be patient. Be

kind. Expect setbacks. *Never strike your dog no matter how frustrated or impatient you become (especially with a newspaper)!* Your pet is always anxious to please. Work with your pet to correct problem behavior and praise the behavior that pleases you. An obedient well-behaved dog is a good friend, family member and community citizen as well as a positive reflection on his responsible pet owner.

WHO SHOULD DO THE TRAINING?

One person should be in charge of training especially when getting started. It helps avoid confusion and

> *"One person should be in charge of training especially when getting started."*

conflicting signals at a critical time. Obedience training requires an adult's sure and strong hand, even if only in a supervisory role. There are potential problems, such as dog fights and dog bites, that require an adult's better judgment, strength and mobility.

Don't expect too much from young children. How much they can help depends on their age, maturity and physical capabilities.

PRAISE AND CORRECTION

Praise or reward for following commands or demonstrating the proper manners is the basis of obedience training. Praise is usually an enthusiastic compliment such as "Good dog" or "Good Fido," enthusiastic stroking or loving petting. Rewards are usually tasty tidbits. Every time you praise or reward your dog, you are teaching him to repeat *whatever* he just did. Praise and reward are big motivators of pets and people.

A correction is a signal to the dog that he did not obey a command or conduct himself properly. Traditional corrections include a stern tug of the leash or a firm scolding. *There should NEVER be any pain or physical punishment connected with a correction.* Pain and punishment are inhumane and ineffective training methods.

TRAINING TIPS

Seek the help of professionals. Having a properly trained, well-behaved dog is too important to be left to chance. Seek the help of professional trainers and veterinarians and educate yourself with formal obedience or training classes, videos and books.

Train in a quiet, confined place. Make sure it is free of distractions for both of you.

Keep the lesson short. This is so you and your puppy will not get tired, bored or frustrated.

Train routinely. Keep a regular schedule.

Train consistently. Use the same tones and commands every time.

Stop destructive or annoying habits early. Jumping up, barking or begging may seem cute as a puppy, but are down right annoying or intolerable as an adult.

Keep commands simple and teach one command at a time.

Use your pet's name before each command. This gets his attention.

Train firmly. Remember, your puppy is a baby with a short attention span and is full of mischief. If he fails to obey a command, repeat it.

Respond immediately. Praise or correct immediately following your dog's response to your command.

Maintain a good attitude. Be enthusiastic and patient.

End with a happy note.

Always play after the lesson is over. Training should be a pleasant experience for both of you.

HOUSETRAINING OR PAPER TRAINING YOUR PUPPY

Teaching your dog to eliminate in the proper place is probably the most important lesson he'll receive and it's something you need to get started with from day one. Crate training is your best chance of having a dog that is happy, healthy and housetrained.

Seven steps to housetrain your pet properly:

1) **Know your pet's**

"Praise and reward are big motivators of pets and people."

EIGHT VALUABLE LESSONS I LEARNED FROM MY DOG

1) Have boundless energy and enthusiasm.
2) Be non-judgmental.
3) Live life for the present.
4) Loyalty is important.
5) Be trusting.
6) Interdependence brings power; we work best as a pack (team).
7) Bury bones for a rainy day.
8) Only the lead dog gets a change of scenery.

by Marty Becker, DVM

schedule. Feed and exercise your dog on a consistent schedule and he'll eliminate predictably. Take your puppy out first thing in the morning, after naps, upon your returning home to your dog that's been left alone, before you go to bed and as soon as the pup gives you "the look!"

2) **Know when your pet has to go.** They will circle, sit and whine at the door or give you the look: anxious, sustained eye contact.

3) **Make sure your pet has a proper diet.** No milk, scraps or people food, period. Feed the same food consistently. Dogs don't need or appreciate variety. Certain premium foods are much more digestible than lower quality foods, thus there is far less stool to eliminate. Ask your veterinarian for details on what to feed.

4) **Seek proper veterinary care.** Internal parasites, or worms, can cause uncontrollable diarrhea and unvaccinated pets are susceptible to many infectious and potentially fatal diseases.

5) **Use odor neutralizers.** You can't just cover up the smell, you have to eliminate it. Your dog's sense of smell is much more acute than ours and he'll return to the same spot again and again until you eliminate the odor. You may also have to use a combination of odor neutralizers, deodorizers and repellants. Don't use ammonia cleaners since ammonia and urine are chemically very similar and smell the same. Remember the smell of diapers? Don't forget to let the area dry thoroughly.

6) **Use proper confinement.** Remember the concept of the den? Dogs hesitate to soil their den. Using this to our benefit, crate training often works wonders.

7) **Use appropriate praises, rewards and corrections.** If your dog

eliminates in the proper place, praise and reward him. If, and only if, you catch him in the act of urinating or defecating inappropriately correct him with a verbal scolding "NO," and immediately take him outside where he was supposed to go to finish. *Don't* hit him, scream at him or rub his nose in it.

Paper training may be better for small dogs, for pet owners who live in high-rise apartments or for those who have difficulty taking their pet outside regularly. This method works best with small females because males lift their leg. Be cautioned, however, once you paper train your pet, it is very difficult to housetrain him otherwise.

CONSTRUCTIVE CHEWING

Puppies lose their baby teeth between the ages of three to six months and have an intense urge to chew. They aren't picky chewers, they don't care or understand if it is your shoes or the chair leg. Chewing behavior is not meant to be destructive. This strong instinctive urge to chew actually helps to keep gums healthy and teeth clean.

To discourage destructive chewing, encourage constructive chewing. Give your puppy safe chew toys such as those made out of nylon, such as Nylabone®,or rope, such as Nylafloss®. Don't give them old socks or shoes or they'll think all socks and shoes are fair game.

Don't give real bones because they can splinter, lodge in the intestinal tract and even cause death. Make the toy "attractive" verbally. When he chews the wrong item a stern "No" should suffice. Also make sure valuable, irreplaceable or potentially dangerous items are inaccessible.

Dog Bone Recipe

MA BARKER'S COOKIES
2 eggs, beaten
3 tablespoons molasses
$\frac{1}{4}$ cup vegetable oil
$\frac{1}{4}$ cup milk
1 cup rolled oats
$\frac{3}{4}$ cup wheat germ
$\frac{1}{4}$ cup whole wheat flour
$\frac{1}{2}$ cup raisins or $\frac{1}{2}$ cup artificial bacon
bits (optional)

Mix ingredients and drop, by teaspoon , on a lightly greased baking sheet. Bake for 15 minutes at 350° F. Remove and allow cookies to dry until crunchy. Once dry, keep in an air-tight container.

OPTIONAL: for added fun, get doggie shaped or bone shaped cookie cutters and let the kids help!

Your Pet's Health

You can do several things to help your pet live life to its fullest potential:

1) **Engage in regular exercise.** Puppies are normally frisky and energetic and need a lot of exercise. Exercise can be a combination of running, brisk walking, swimming, fetching and playing. It's good for you too! The amount of exercise depends mostly on the breed rather than the size of the dog. Remember your dog will need regular daily exercise throughout his life to be happy and healthy.

2) **Conduct regular checkups at home.** Just shoving the food under your dog's face and walking away isn't being a responsible, caring, loving pet owner. Your dog requires a daily dose of love and attention. I recommend giving the pet a vitamin as both a treat and a "daily dose of love." Use the vitamin as a catalyst to spend a few minutes with your pet each day, to examine him and get him used to being handled. Some pet owners intuitively know when their pet is sick but with a new puppy or sometimes with an "old friend" it is difficult to know when something is wrong. Here are a few indicators that something is wrong: loss of appetite, sudden weight loss or prolonged gradual weight loss, sluggishness or unwillingness to play or exercise, excessive thirst, overly frequent or difficult urination, bloody, mucousy or unformed stools, persistent vomiting, excessive salivation, bad breath, persistent cough, irregular or labored breathing, dull dry coat, lumps on or under the skin, runny eyes, foul-smelling ears, etc. Your dog's normal temperature is 100-102 degrees. If you are careful, you can check it with a rectal thermometer lubricated with petroleum jelly.

3) **Practice good grooming habits.** All dogs need grooming. Grooming is natural to dogs, as in the wild they groom each other. Regular grooming not only

keeps your pet handsome but it also removes dead hair, dirt and parasites. Start right away so that your pet becomes comfortable with being handled. This will also help when your pet needs to stand quietly for the veterinarian, groomer or for your home health checkups. Start grooming in short sessions. Talk to your pet gently and treat him gently. If he wiggles or fights, sternly say "No." If

he's still, praise him. Make sure that you take your dog to a professional groomer or use specialized pet grooming equipment and supplies. Human products can actually harm your pet. Bathe your pet only as needed. Too many baths can strip your puppy's coat of essential oils.

4) **Practice preventive health care.** Vaccinations are an essential part of a good health maintenance

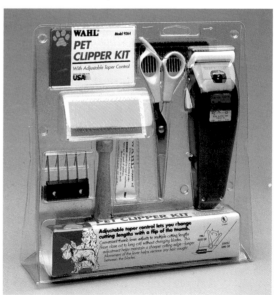

Left: Regular grooming is a key ingredient to successful flea control. The new age design of the Innomed Groom 'N Flea pet comb from Interplex allows the comb head to lock in one of the three different positions. **Below:** Grooming kits, such as the Pet Clipper Kit by Wahl, are economical and available in pet stores.

GREAT GROOMING TIPS

The amount and type of routine grooming you must do on your dog depend a lot on the type of dog you own. For example, Golden Retrievers require a lot of brushing, Poodles usually require professional grooming and Dachshunds require very little grooming.

Like humans, pets require certain things that keep them clean, odor free and looking their best. Although pets do a lot of their own grooming, they still need our help with the following things:

1) Longhaired dogs need to be brushed frequently.
2) Nails need to be kept short (dewclaws too).
3) Long-eared dogs need to have their ears cleaned.
4) Teeth need to be brushed daily and given therapeutic chews.
5) Bathe as needed (with a pet shampoo).
6) In flea areas, make sure your pet is safe from these troublemakers!

"The amount and type of grooming you must do on your dog depend on the type of dog you own."

47

program for your dog. They provide immunity from highly contagious diseases that can jeopardize the life of your pet. Even dogs that have little or no contact with other animals need protection since diseases spread rapidly through indirect contact. It is important that the puppy be vaccinated early, since his maternal immunity diminishes just as he's undergoing the stress of being weaned and moved to a new home. In addition, some of these diseases, such as rabies and leptospirosis, may be hazardous to people. Just as important are regular programs of external-parasite control (e.g., fleas, ticks), internal-parasite control (e.g., roundworms, hookworms, tapeworms), heartworm prevention (i.e., parasites that live in the dog's heart) and nutrition. Ask your veterinarian to outline a personalized preventive health care program for your pet.

PROPER VETERINARY CARE

Proper veterinary care is fundamental and vital to your pet's physical and psychological health and will help protect your unique and precious human/animal bond. Your veterinarian is a talented and caring resource dedicated to ensuring that both you and your pet get the most out of your relationship and that your pet is happy, healthy, and lives his life to the fullest.

Today's veterinarians are trained to handle questions from pre-purchase counseling to grievance counseling, including questions on pet selection, husbandry, nutrition, behavioral training, etc. Veterinarians, or the experts they recommend, can help you with everything concerning your pet's welfare and ecosystem. Your veterinarian will encourage your questions because they want you to understand *everything* concerning your pet's care and well-being. Through education, you are better able to understand your veterinarian's recommendations and make informed decisions.

Your veterinarian's goal is the maintenance of health *not* the treatment of illnesses or accidents. The absence of illness is not necessarily an indication of good health. The common goal of you and your

veterinarian is optimum health and well-being for your pet through the practice of wellness programs and preventive health care.

Here are three significant things your veterinarian can do:

1) **Provide expert advice.**

Your veterinarian knows what's best for your pet or he can guide you to experts that do. Together, they can advise and guide you through your pet's life. Think of veterinarians as

"Ask your vet to outline a personalized preventive health care program for your pet."

spokespersons for your pet's best interests.

2) **Schedule regular checkups.** At least once a year, and more often for older dogs, your veterinarian should examine your dog from the tip of his nose to the tip of his tail. They'll also evaluate the internal organ functions by "looking inside your dog" through blood chemistry tests, urinalysis, fecal exams and sometimes radiographs. These sophisticated tests can help to catch problems early on, while they are still treatable or before they cause unnecessary pain, expense... or worse.

3) **Set up preventive health care programs.** Your veterinarian's goal is to minimize health problems and optimize health. They would rather work to maintain good health than try to cure the sick or heal the wounded. Preventive health care programs include vaccinations, parasite control, dentistry, grooming, nutrition and even behavior management. On your puppy's first visit, your veterinarian will probably outline the start programs on vaccinations, worming, flea prevention or

control, heartworms, dental care and proper nutrition. Take this opportunity to ask the veterinarian about healthy treats, neutering or other areas of concern.

REASONS TO SPAY OR NEUTER YOUR PET

The animal population is exploding. Each year millions of unwanted pets are born and most are treated like "living garbage" and are disposed of. Even the pets that avoid euthanasia are condemned to live without homes or without love. This is tragic and reprehensible ... but also preventable.

Spaying and neutering are ways of providing population control for dogs by removing their reproductive organs. Spaying is the procedure for females and neutering refers to the procedure used for males.

Spaying and neutering are good for everyone:

1) **It's good for your dog.** It reduces your dog's desire to roam. It also reduces his risk of certain reproductive cancers and reproductive diseases. For females it eliminates the heat cycle and therefore no more nervousness, bloody

discharge and unwelcome Romeos. For males it stops the mating desire, reduces mounting and the tendency to "go-a-courting." Spayed or neutered pets generally live longer lives.

2) **It's good for you.** There will be no more problems with blood stains, dogs' breaking into your yard, dogs' running away in search of a mate and the task of taking care of and finding homes for an unwanted litter.

3) **It's good for the community.** Homeless pets often create serious problems. They destroy property, spread disease and cost a lot of money to control.

Before you decide to breed your pet, or take the chance of your pet's breeding, consider that:

1) Every hour, more than 2,000 puppies are born. Only two out of ten will find permanent homes.

2) A dog abandoned on

"In males, neutering stops the mating desire, reduces mounting and the tendency to 'go-a-courting.'"

the street has a life expectancy of one year.

3) Only 20% of the animals brought to shelters and pounds are adopted each year. The rest are destroyed!

If you do decide to breed your dog, consider the consequences. Will all the puppies have homes? Are you aware that your dog could die as a result of the pregnancy or delivery? Are you prepared to handle the increased cost of pre- and postnatal care for the mother and expenses for vaccinations, food and grooming for the litter? Are you ready, willing and able to give time, attention and love to mother and her litter? Are you aware that by having a litter, you may be depriving homeless animals of a home?

Educate yourself. Consider the future and the best interests of everyone concerned, then make an informed decision.

Your Dog's Critical First Year

Although every year of your dog's life is important and something to be cherished, your dog's first year of life has extra importance. For it is during this first year of life that your dog develops a strong body, learns basic obedience and develops his unique personality. If you neglect your dog or make mistakes during this critical time, the damage can be difficult to correct or even irreparable.

For example, if you don't provide your puppy with the proper kinds and amounts of food, their teeth, bones and muscles may not fully develop and they may become weak and prone to disease. If you don't teach your dog basic obedience, he may still be eliminating in the house long after he is an adult. And if you don't spend time with your friend and socialize him, he may always be overly timid or extremely aggressive to strangers.

Of all the common mistakes and failures of raising a new puppy, perhaps the most common and serious is the lack of patience or perseverance by the owner. Remember, the puppy is just a baby. And if you have ever raised or been around young children, you know that there are certain things they don't have the ability to understand or learn at first, such as toilet training. The same is true for your puppy with housetraining. So be patient, understanding and responsible, and in time everything will be just fine.

There are four basic things you can do during your pet's first year of life to ensure and enhance his health. We call them the four C's:

1) *Commitment*—A responsibility to look after your pet's best interests ... no matter what.

2) *Care*—You accept the sacrifice of time and money necessary to have a pet who is happy and healthy.

3) *Contact*—The pet is not relegated to "outer space" for life (the backyard on a chain),

"It is during this first year of life that your dog develops a strong body, learns basic obedience and develops his unique personality."

53

but rather is a joyous part of everyday family activity.

4) *Compassion*—The willingness to do anything within your power not only to prevent pain and suffering but to enhance your pet's health and happiness. A conscience!

Dogs are pack animals and your puppy will have to learn that you are the leader of the pack. You must teach your dog that his world revolves around you and your approval is the greatest thing in his world.

As leader of the pack, you maintain the attitude that you are a working team. Show your dog respect and he will show you respect in return. You have the moral obligation to *never, ever* hurt your dog physically or emotionally. The old school of beating or forcing your puppy to conform usually causes fearful, timid, distrusting, aggressive adults.

Your puppy will have five primary needs during his first year of life:

1) Food
2) Water
3) Exercise
4) Loving discipline
5) Love and attention

The first two are basic and quite easily provided. The others are going to require more commitment and work on your part. But you must enthusiastically commit your family to provide for all five needs in adequate amounts or, rest assured, your pet will suffer negative consequences for your failures ... and so will you.

If you feed your pet a high-quality premium dog food, keep plenty of fresh clean water available at all times and exercise him regularly, he will reach adulthood with a strong body that is resistant to infection and ready for strenuous play.

And just as importantly, if you have taught your puppy the rules he needs to live by through basic obedience training and have given him unconditional love and copious amounts of attention, then he will be ready, willing and able to take his place as a loved and loving member of the family. Just remember to praise positive behavior and not dwell on negative behavior. Try to catch your pet doing things right—not doing things wrong!

When It Comes Time To Say Good-Bye

A sad reality about the blessing of the human/animal bond is that it is only forever in memory. The death of a pet is a painful but inevitable ordeal.

Crying and depression are normal responses to the death of a significant friend, whether human or animal. Your feelings and emotions should not be suppressed and you shouldn't feel ashamed. Acknowledge that it hurts and it's all right to be upset. This will help.

In due time your emotions will run their course and you'll be okay. If you're having trouble coping, or have persistent depression, join support groups, talk to sympathetic or trained ears or get books or videotapes on the subject. Ask your veterinarian for recommendations. Sometimes a burial or memorial service helps too.

What should you tell your child when a pet dies? Follow two simple rules: tell the truth and empathize with them. Children will know or figure out that explanations such as "He just ran away" are untrue or they may even feel that it's their fault. If the dog must be euthanized, explain it as "Fido was so sick that he started to die. We didn't want him to suffer. We helped speed things up, so he wouldn't suffer anymore."

A Dog's Prayer

by Beth Norman Harris

Treat me kindly, my beloved master, for no heart in all the world is more grateful for kindness than the loving heart of me.

Do not break my spirit with a stick, for though I should lick your hand between the blows, your patience and understanding will more quickly teach me the things you would have me do.

Speak to me often, for your voice is the world's sweetest music, as you must know by the fierce wagging of my tail when your footstep falls upon my waiting ear.

When it is cold and wet, please take me inside, for I am now a domesticated animal, no longer used to bitter elements. And I ask no greater glory than the privilege of sitting at your feet beside the hearth. Though had you no home, I would rather follow you through ice and snow than rest upon the softest pillow in the warmest home in all the land, for you are my god and I am your devoted worshiper.

If you are having trouble coping with the death of your pet, a burial or memorial service sometimes helps.

Keep my pan filled with fresh water, for although I should not reproach you were it dry, I cannot tell you when I suffer thirst. Feed me clean food, that I may stay well, to romp and play and do your bidding, to walk by your side, and stand ready, willing and able to protect you with my life should your life be in danger.

And, beloved master, should the Great master see fit to deprive me of my health or sight, do not turn me away from you. Rather, hold me gently in your arms as skilled hands grant me merciful boon of eternal rest—and I will leave you knowing with the last breath I drew, my fate was ever safest in your hands.

Checklists for a Happy and Healthy Puppy

The crate should be just big enough to permit a grown dog to stand and stretch.

ABSOLUTE NECESSITIES

1) Premium foods (100% guaranteed)
2) Bowls (food and water)
3) Leash and collar or leash and harness
4) ID tag and microchip
5) Pet carrier or crate (appropriate size for adults) and grill floor
6) Housetraining aids
7) Therapeutic chew toys (Nylabone®, Gumabone® and Nylafloss®)
8) Stain remover and odor eliminator
9) Repellents and/or chew stops
10) Shampoo and conditioner
11) Brush or comb
12) Ear cleansing solution for long-eared and problem-eared dogs
13) Flea and tick control products
14) Toothbrush kit and other dental aids
15) Obedience training (formal classes, books, videos, etc.)
16) Schedule exam with veterinarian (for vaccinations, worming, heart worm check, physical, etc.)
17) Loving, responsible, informed pet ownership

HIGHLY RECOMMENDED ITEMS OR SERVICES

1) Dog treats (Chooz™)
2) Nail trimmer and styptic preparation (blood stopper)
3) Pooper scooper
4) Dog house
5) Tie out (cable, trolley or chain)
6) Air tight food container and scoop
7) Insurance (major medical and accident)
8) Regular grooming program (clipping and/or bathing)
9) Resting cushion or bed

OTHER SUGGESTED ITEMS

1) Pet hair pickup
2) Dog door
3) Portable pen
4) Pressure gate (to confine pet to parts of the house)
5) Kennel heater (if outdoors)
6) Books on dog care and breed references
7) Cologne spray
8) Cream rinse or de-tangling spray
9) Sanitary pants and pads for bitches in heat
10) Tear stain remover
11) Sweaters
12) Rug and room deodorizer
13) Automatic waterer

DAILY CHECKLIST

Please use this pet health checklist on a regular basis. We suggest at least monthly. You can help discover many problems early on, before they cause unnecessary pain, expenses... or worse.

MY PET:

1) is acting normal, active and in good spirits.
2) does not tire easily with moderate exercise.
3) does not have seizures or fainting episodes.
4) has a normal appetite, with no significant weight change.
5) does not vomit or regurgitate his food.
6) has normal appearing bowel movements (firm, formed, mucos-free).
7) doesn't drag his bottom or chew under the tail excessively.
8) has a full, glossy coat with no missing hair, no matts or excessive shedding.
9) doesn't scratch, lick or chew itself excessively.
10) has skin that is free from dry flakes, is not greasy, and has no bad odor.
11) is free from fleas, ticks, lice or mites.
12) has a body that is free from lumps or bumps.
13) has ears that are clean and odor free.
14) doesn't shake his head or dig at his ears.
15) has eyes that are bright, clear, and free of matter.
16) has normal hearing and reactions to his environment.
17) walks without stiffness, pain, or difficulty.
18) has healthy-looking feet and short nails (dewclaws too).
19) breathes normally, without straining or coughing.
20) has normal thirst and drinks in the usual amount and frequency.
21) urinates in the usual amounts and frequency; color is normal.

22) has a moist nose, free from discharge.
23) has clean, white teeth, free from plaque, tartar or bad breath.
24) has gums that are pink with no redness, swelling or offensive breath odor.
25) has no offensive habits (biting, barking, digging, chewing, scratching, spraying).
26) is well housetrained.

REMEMBER THESE RULES:

1) Your pet should wear a collar and complete identification tag including pet's name and your name, address and telephone number. Your pet should be implanted with a microchip. This

Chooz™ are edible treats for dogs made from cheese protein and chicken.

is permanent and discourages theft.

2) If you take your animal out, remember to use a leash.

3) When riding with your pet in a car, keep the windows rolled up high enough so he cannot jump out.

4) During busy times, such as holidays and parties, be extra careful. Lots of people and activity in the house can cause your pet to become overexcited and bolt through an open door. It is best to keep your pet confined to a quiet room of the house during these times.

5) Remember to keep current photographs of your pet.

IF YOUR PET IS LOST:

1) Check the neighborhood first. Often pets don't stray too far from

Nylabone® and Gumabone® dog pacifiers have proven effective in the control of tartar and tooth decay in dogs.

Nylafloss® is equipped with individual nylon strands that help remove tartar from between dogs' teeth. Gently tugging and playing with your dog with the Nylafloss® reduces the chances of periodontal disease and other mouth disorders.

home. Use a photograph to check if anyone has seen your pet.

2) Let everyone know your pet is missing: veterinary hospitals, neighborhood children, newspaper delivery person, mail carrier, neighbors, joggers, etc.

3) Visit your local animal shelter to see if your pet has been brought there.

4) Use your photograph and photocopy it. Include the pet's name and information on color, breed, sex and your name and telephone number. Then place flyers in high-traffic areas, such as supermarkets, drug stores, dry cleaners, veterinary hospitals and other area merchants.

Doggie Scrapbook

Pet's Name _____

Nickname _____

Here's how I came up with the name _____

_____

Where I got my dog _____

How I picked out this special dog _____

_____

My dog weighed this much when I first brought him/her home _____

Special markings _____

Favorite place to be scratched or pet _____

Favorite treat _____

Favorite toy _____

A unique story about my dog _____

_____

_____

_____

The funniest thing my dog ever did _____

_____

My dog's tricks _____

My dog's best friend _____

My dog's worst enemy _____

All-Breed Dog Books From T.F.H.

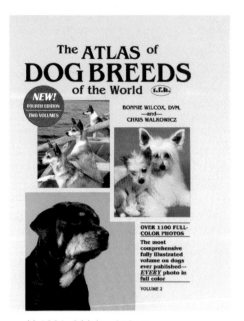

The ATLAS of
DOG BREEDS
of the World

NEW! FOURTH EDITION TWO VOLUMES

BONNIE WILCOX, DVM,
—and—
CHRIS WALKOWICZ

OVER 1100 FULL-COLOR PHOTOS

The most comprehensive fully illustrated volume on dogs ever published--- *EVERY* photo in full color

VOLUME 2

H-1106, 544 pp
Over 400 color photos

H-1091, 2 Vols., 912 pp
Over 1100 color photos

The T.F.H. all-breed dog books are the most comprehensive and colorful of all dog books available. The most famous of these recent publications, *The Atlas of Dog Breeds of the World,* written by Dr. Bonnie Wilcox and Chris Walkowicz, is now available as a two-volume set. Now in its fourth edition, the *Atlas* remains one of the most sought-after gift books and reference works in the dog world.

A very successful spinoff of the *Atlas* is the *Mini-Atlas of Dog Breeds,* written by Andrew De Prisco and James B. Johnson. This compact but comprehensive book has been praised and recommended by most national dog publications for its utility and reader-friendliness. It is the true field guide for dog lovers.

TS-175, 896 pp
Over 1300 color photos

Canine Lexicon by the authors of the *Mini-Atlas* is an up-to-date encyclopedic dictionary for the dog person. It is the most complete single volume on the dog ever published, covering more breeds than any other book as well as other relevant topics, including health, showing, training, breeding, anatomy, veterinary terms, and much more. No dog book before has ever offered this many stunning color photographs of all breeds, dog sports, and topics. (over 1300 in full color!).

More Dog Books From T.F.H. Publications, Inc.

t.f.h.

H-1016, 224 pp
135 photos

H-969, 224 pp
62 color photos

H-1061, 608 pp
Black/white photos

TS-101, 192 pp
Over 100 photos

TW-102, 256 pp
Over 200 color

TW-113, 256 pp
200 color photos

H-962, 255 pp
Nearly 100 photos

SK-044, 64 pp
Over 50 color
photos

PS-872, 240 pp
78 color illustrations

H-1095, 272 pp
Over 160 color illustrations

INDEX